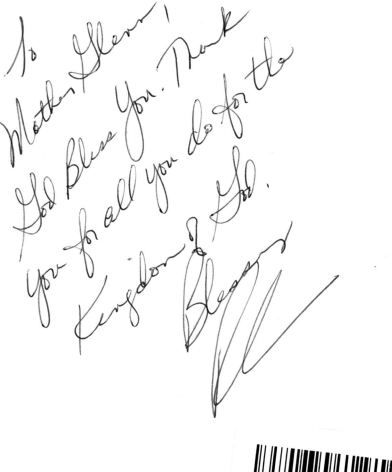

To
Mother Glenn,
God Bless You. Thank
You for all you do for the
Kingdom of God.
Blessings

D1496532

Sunless SKIES

How to Release the Sorrow of Grief

ROSETTA ARCHER

WITH A FOREWORD BY KEITH A. BUTLER

Rosetta Archer
P.O. Box 7794 • Bloomfield Hills, MI 48302
Sunless.skies@gmail.com

Sunless SKIES

How to Release the Sorrow of Grief

ROSETTA ARCHER

FOREWORD BY KEITH A. BUTLER

Sunless SKIES

How to Release the Sorrow of Grief
ROSETTA ARCHER

Unless otherwise indicated, all Scripture quotations are taken from the King James Version of the Holy Bible.

ISBN: 978-0-9899386-0-0
ISBN (eBook): 978-0-9899386-1-7

Library of Congress Copyright
Control#: 1-350858851
Copyright © 2013 by Rosetta Archer

Published by:

Sunless SKIES, LLC
P.O. Box 7794 • Bloomfield Hills, MI 48302
Sunless.skies@gmail.com
Sunless SKIES also available on eBook

Graphic Designer, Andrea Simpson
Simpson Communications, simpsoncommunicationsa.com
Cover Photography Courtesy of shutterstock.com

Dedication

To all those who have lost loved ones;

to every Counselor, Pastor, Minister, Elder,

Reverend, Priest, Chaplain, Physician,

Rabbi, Teacher, Abba,

Neighbor, Friend, Colleague

and the Individuals who help them.

Contents

Part IV: Short-Term Separation

Acknowledgements

John Donne coined the phrase: *"No man is an island."* Those words are so true. The person I am, the skills, talents and abilities I possess, have come as a result of so many people taking the time to pour their gifts into me. It goes without saying that God has the ultimate plan for man. He has used many, many people to smooth my rough edges to uncover this beautiful diamond in the rough. Thank you for the time and patience you have invested in me.

To my amazing husband George. Your love, integrity and patience are second to none. Thank you for your unwavering love and support. I will always love you.

To Life's Perfect Parents, Theodore Roosevelt and Luella Wilkins Davis. It is crystal clear that God blessed me with Life's Perfect Parents. People always say, "Nobody's perfect", but you were. You always lived by the principles you taught. You taught me to Love God, Love Our Family, Love and Help Others and to Love Myself. As you both rest in the arms of Jesus, I am so grateful for your life and legacy. With long life you were satisfied, and the life you lived is still motivating and blessing others. I look forward to our heavenly reunion. Thank you for EVERYTHING!

To my sister Jackie, you have come through great trials and tribulations; you've come through the fire and the flood, but you made it! You are my best supporter and greatest cheerleader.

To Pastor Andre and Min. Tiffany; God has a future for us.

To my church family; Word of Faith International Christian Center, Faith Christian Center and Faith-4Life Church.

To Harvey Lee, Faith, Charity, Benjamin, Marcus, Christina Joy, Stephen, LaTina, Darrin, Brenetta, MiChelle and Kristina. The joy that has come from watching you grow from a dream to wonderful young men and women is indescribable. I'm proud of you all.

To the worlds greatest friends and prayer partners, Mark and LaTonya Jackson, Dr. Robert and Melestine Garner and Atty. Robyn Brooks. Words could never describe the strength and stamina you have given me.

To Andrew and Verlinda, Andrea Simpson, Dale and Carla, Curtis, the Donaldson Family; the Adams Family and the Walker's; you are the best. Thanks for doing life together with me.

To those who read this book, thank you in advance.

You will not be disappointed.

To Andrea Simpson and Simpson Communications; there is no graphic designer or instructor more talented on the face of the earth than you. You are indeed the best. Thank you for everything.

To Rev. Ronald Pritchett, wherever you are. Thank you for pulling countless people from the black hole of grief up to the shining light of hope.

To my fabulous feedback team (FFT): Cathy, Cheryl, Diane, Shronda, LaTonya, Lois, Al, Charity, Victor and Johnnie. What a blessing you are.

To Christina Dixon of Priority One Publications, Venus Mason Theus of Anointed Pen, and Dr. Kimberley Savage; thank you.

To Delmar Mays, the bookseller of all booksellers. Your words have propelled this book in ways you will never know. Thank you for your sensitivity and wisdom.

To Steve Arterburn; thanks for helping millions of people navigate life's greatest challenges.

To Dr. Marilyn Hickey; the blessing you prayed over me is still producing fruit.

To Rev. Kate McVeigh; thank you for always encouraging me and teaching the world how to walk in Favor.

To Bishop George and Pastor April Davis; I love you.

To Dr. J. Victor and Min. Catherine Eagan, thank you for your wisdom.

To my family, the Archer's, the Hester's, the Carnegie's, the Barkers, the Middleton's, and the Wynn's.

To my spiritual parents and beyond, Bishop Keith and Pastor Deborah Butler; a million words could never express my love, admiration, appreciation and gratitude. Only God is wealthy enough to reward you for the seeds you have planted in my life.

To the only wise God our Savior, be glory and majesty, dominion and power, both now and forever more. You are Greater, Stronger and Higher than any other. I love you more than anything.

Foreword

by Keith A. Butler

Unfortunately, experiencing grief is a part of life. As a Senior Pastor for over 30 years, I have counseled many grieving families. Some have been under tragic circumstances. There have been infants, toddlers, teenagers, young adults and those from middle age to senior citizens.

Sunless SKIES is a valuable resource for those experiencing grief. It also includes tools and practical applications to help you help someone else who may be grieving. The information is presented in a clear, concise format, sure to help the reader gain insight and wisdom to move through the grieving process.

As you read through these pages, you will receive a greater understanding of the grieving process, and more importantly, you will learn how to apply the information. It is my prayer that you be strengthened with His might as you navigate your sunless skies.

Keith A. Butler is the Founder and President of Keith Butler Ministries; he is also the Senior Pastor of Faith4Life Church Dallas, TX. Rev. Butler is also the Founder & Presiding Bishop of Word of Faith Int'l Christian Center Church in Southfield, MI.

Introduction

According to the most recent statistics available from the National Mental Health Association, in the U. S., eight million people suffered through the death of someone in their immediate family last year. That number does not include the extended family relationships like in-laws, aunts, uncles, nieces, nephews, cousins, blended family or step-relationships and others. Research by the late Dr. Elizabeth Weller, Director of Ohio State University Hospitals, suggests that 1.2 million children will lose a parent to death before age 15.

With so much pain and anguish due to the death of family, friends, co-workers and associates, there is no questioning that, eventually, grief will come knocking at your door. When grief comes to you, someone you care about, or those you are connected to, are you prepared to handle the pain, anguish and emotional pressure that often accompanies it? Are you positioned to help someone who may be suffering the pains of grief as a result of a loss?

After a significant loss, it is normal to grieve. For many the pain and loss seems too much to bear and impossible to heal. Believing that no one else in this world could possibly understand the grief and sense of loss you are facing is common. A long illness, the sudden death of a spouse, child, or parent, in addition to many other losses, can seem insurmountable. Even if you felt there was a slim chance you could be helped, you cannot imagine where you would begin the healing process. After all, the pain is so deep and constant, it hurts everywhere.

Grief knows no boundaries of age, race, gender, education, social or economic status. However, you must move through the grieving process. Staying in a perpetual state of grief and sorrow will choke the very life out of you, if you allow it. So, where do you begin? If you could somehow begin, how long would it take? Will the pain ever end? You must tackle it head on. But how do you do that?

If you identify with these feelings, here is some good news: there is help, and there is hope. The purpose of this practical reference is to assist those who are suffering the pains of grief by answering many of your questions and help you work through your grief. There are countless others hurting from situations and circumstances just as painful as yours or the person you are assisting. Their true stories will remind you that you are not alone.

Introduction

As you read through these pages, it is our hope that the words and practical applications will encourage you and help you heal from your loss and give you a sense of hope. Apply the principles outlined, utilize the self-help resources and you will move from sunless skies to brighter days ahead. Not only that, the day will come when you will be able to help someone else. If you are not the one grieving, this book will provide tools that can be utilized to help those who are struggling to release the sorrow of grief.

My Story

"Your mother has six to eight hours to live."

T he day before Mother died, someone from the hospital left a business card from the Palliative Care Department. I did not think too much about it because I did not know what Palliative Care was. Anyway, various hospital staff had come and left business cards. This day was not much different than the past two days.

As was my custom, I went to visit Mother in the hospital. She was admitted a week or so earlier, and from what we could tell, she was on the mend. Sure, she had experienced better days, but this day did not appear different. I finally asked someone what was the Palliative Care Department. I should have known by the look on her face something was amiss. She said very carefully, *"They deal with end of life."* My first thought was, *"That's strange, why would they leave this card in my mother's room?"* I honestly didn't think twice about it. I counted it as a mistake, and contin-

5

ued on as usual. I sat with her, prayed with her and visited with her.

The next day, I noticed more hospital personnel gathered in and around my mother's room than normal. Some would peek in and go back out. After a number of times, I decided to investigate. I stepped into the hall and asked, *"Is everything okay?"* One of the lead hospital physicians started talking in a manner I would describe as *"spastic."* He was so nervous. Finally, I said,

"Hold it. Are you trying to tell me something?" He hesitated and then began scrambling for words. I said,

"Listen, I can handle it, just tell me." He literally blurted out:

"Your mother has six to eight hours to live."

I did not say it out loud, but on the inside I said, *"What? Oh no, you are mistaken. My mother will live forever."*

I certainly did not expect to hear those words. Apparently, the hospital staff knew that she was dying, but we, the family, had no clue. I had to make a decision right then and there not to be angry or drowned by grief. There were so many issues, feelings and questions that flooded me at that moment. However, I knew I could not allow grief to take control of or consume my life. I was determined to fight it tooth and nail.

Mere words could never adequately describe what it was like selecting a coffin for mother. If that were not painful enough, we had the task of going through her clothes as we decided what she would wear in her coffin. Every garment with a memory attached. Should we just buy something new? How about having to write an obituary in the midst of more emotions than you ever thought possible?

If you have not been touched by the loss of someone you love, the day will come. As the old folks used to say: *"Just keep living."* As a result of reading and applying this information, you will be better prepared and equipped to help yourself and someone else get through the process when it comes.

Several years ago I was attending a memorial service at a particular church where they needed someone to sing. I was the only person available. As I sat in the service, watching the grieving family, seeing their tears, hearing their cries, I began to feel quite heavy and sorrowful myself. I did not know the deceased, but all the sadness somehow consumed me as well. All of a sudden, something happened that I could not explain at the time.

The minister opened his Bible, read a few scriptures and then talked directly to the immediate family. He told them how life was not over, and how their loved one was rejoicing. He talked about Heaven, and he told them not to feel sorry for their loved one who had *"gone on."* He said if you want to feel sorry for someone, feel sorry for those of us still here. We are the ones still in this rat race. We are the ones still paying bills and working hard. We are the ones still dealing with all the issues of life.

To my amazement, he took the family from heavy sorrow in tears and wailing, to shouts of joy and thanksgiving. Family after family, service after service, week in and week out. His message always the same with the same result: families would enter depressed and discouraged, but they'd exit with a newfound hope and peace.

For years, I listened to him talk about heaven and all its greatness. He told the families how one day all sorrow would end, and to be thankful for the time spent with their loved one, whether long or short. Little did I realize, I was being fortified because my *day of grieving* would come following the sudden death of my mother. Even today there are times her death seems like a bad dream. I did not realize it at the time, but what happened that day would be the catalyst for this book. Since the day Mother died, I have been on a mission to help people struggling with grief. This book and all the principles outlined, has been compiled to help as many people as possible ease the pain and suffering that a significant loss may bring.

The Journey

"They think my brother was on that plane."

He was phenomenal. He would sing until heaven touched earth, and then the Pastor would preach until heaven came down again. He was full of life, full of joy and full of music. When I heard one of my closest friends and music mentor was suddenly killed in an airplane crash, I couldn't believe my ears.

When I arrived at church for mid-week service there were people walking the halls praying and crying, though I did not notice them at the time. In fact, it did not strike me as strange because we always encouraged everyone to "come in and pray." I went to our normal meeting place where the atmosphere was rather somber. Shortly, my friend's sister rushed into the room without speaking to me. That was certainly unusual. She was a close friend too and always greeted me. Puzzled by the lack of communication I looked at her and said,

"Hey." She looked very stern so I asked,
"What's the matter?"

"They think my brother was on that plane," she responded.

"What plane?" I asked. She said,
"The one that crashed."

All I could think was somehow she was mistaken. Although I wanted to be sensitive and not lambaste her, I needed clarification. I quickly decided to look for someone else who could make sense out of what she said. Finally someone arrived who I was confident would know the facts. The person confirmed what my friend had told me. Although the individual could always be trusted to give accurate information, I still did not want to believe the report. It just could not be true.

While driving home from work before heading to the church service, I stayed tuned to the radio. When I arrived home, my eyes were glued to the television. At that particular time, I was working for a major airline. Once the airline office manager announced the airplane incident, it was hard for me to concentrate. The news was just heartbreaking. As a matter of fact, I was almost late for my reporting time for church service because of watching all the news coverage.

Never in a million years did I think I knew someone on the aircraft. However, it turned out that I did. I remember calling the airline hotline for information and also trying to get information about the flight manifest. *"Surely, there must be a mistake."* But there was no mistake. Indeed he was on the flight.

That incident changed many lives forever, including mine. He was flying as the guest musician and psalmist for a conference. He loved to travel with his Pastor. Sure, there have been others who have passed, but this one was particularly painful. A wife lost a husband, a mother lost a son; children lost a father, siblings lost a brother, many lost a friend; the world lost an amazing man of valor.

Part 1
Grief
Principles

Chapter 1

What is Grief?

When navigating the tempestuous emotions of grief, it is important to understand what grief is. As with any resource, in order to obtain maximum results, you must understand the topic being covered. *Grief* is defined by *Noah Webster's 1828 American Dictionary of the English Language* as *the pain produced by loss, misfortune, injury or evils of any kind; sorrow; regret; that which afflicts; to make sorrowful; to wound the feelings; to feel pain of mind or heart.* Simply put, grief is the feeling or sense of **loss**.

Many situations can cause grief. Some people grieve because they have lost a pet, a job, a dream, or a relationship. There are certainly parallels that can be drawn concerning these areas. However, our concentration is grief caused by loss of human life.

Feelings of Loss

"My mother left me an orphan."

After a significant loss, many times people feel abandoned and all alone. I know of a young man who is an only child. When his beautiful mother passed away suddenly he said, "My mother left me an orphan." Because he had no siblings, he felt a greater sense of loss. Fortunately, he has a strong support system helping him heal from the hurt associated with his mother's passing.

There are many reasons for loss of human life. They include people who die as a result of long or short term illnesses; transportation accidents including automobile, motorcycle, bus, train, aircraft and water crafts; those who serve in the military and protective services; victims of crime and mistaken identity. There are medical errors, suicide; miscarriage, abortion and sudden death to name a few. No matter the reason for our loss, there is help.

After a significant loss, many people are faced with circumstances they never imagined. Many are left caretakers, single parents or the sole bread winner. For those who die without wills or life insurance, a huge financial burden may be added to the already stressful life changes. Regardless of the circumstances you face, there is hope. You can work through your feelings of loss.

Chapter 2

Why We Grieve

hy do we grieve? That is a very important question. We grieve because we have suffered a significant loss. We are no longer able to touch, smell, hear, and see someone we loved or whose company we enjoyed. The one we birthed or fathered; the one who birthed or fathered us; the person who listened to us, or to whom we listened; the one who helped us or made us laugh; the one who motivated or held us accountable; our mentor, our friend, our nemesis, our sibling, our neighbor; the one who played with us, purchased things for us. How about those that greeted us at work, the store, the theatre, or the gas station? The list goes on and on.

Regardless of the place they held in our lives, the bottom line is the same: they can no longer be *"touched"* with our senses. Even though we may or may not have communicated with them daily, weekly or even monthly, death brings about undeniable finality. The pain of physical separation cannot be avoided. However, you can and must make the decision to continue living. Over time, your grieving process should come to an end.

Personal Notes

Personal Notes

Personal Notes

_____

_____

_____

_____

_____

_____

_____

_____

_____

_____

_____

Part 2
Grief
Cycles

Chapter 3

How is Grief Expressed?

There is no *right* way to grieve. Grieving is very personal. Everyone is different. Not all people will grieve the same, and that is okay. Often people take the position and say that if someone does not cry, get angry, or become an emotional wreck, that person is in denial. That is not necessarily the case. On the contrary, there are those who grieve quietly, almost silently. Yes, some people may be in denial, but let's not be judgmental. Let us identify ways to help them, and go from there.

Ways People Grieve

1. Denial–Some people pretend or function as if nothing has changed. They do not acknowledge their significant loss.
2. Isolation–Some people do not want to talk to or be around anyone. They just want to be left alone.
3. Anger–Some people become extremely angry at

the world, angry at God, angry at anything that moves, and sometimes things that don't move.

4. Vices–Some people launch head forward into drinking, drugging, and carousing; anything to "drown their sorrows" and "take the pain away."

5. Blame–Some people blame themselves and they blame others: "If I had done this or that..." "If you had only done..."

6. Calm confidence–Some people really understand that death is a part of life and are able to grieve in a calm manner. They put life and death in its proper perspective very quickly. They are able to recognize the good and the bad. They adjust in a relatively short period of time. This is more likely to occur when someone has lived a long fulfilling life. Although you never want a loved one to leave you, when they have lived long and well, it makes the bitter pill of death slightly easier to swallow.

7. Melting Pot–Some do a combination of this list as well as other things not listed.

Regardless of how you express your grief, it is important to move through the grieving process in a positive, effective manner. You will learn tools and techniques to help you as you continue reading.

Chapter 4

Stages of Grief

There are basic stages of grief. The stages listed are not the only ones, but they are the basic ones. Each stage has its own nuances. Each stage could be a book of its own so we will not go into great detail. Dr. Elizabeth Kubler-Ross outlines the basic stages of grief in her book, *On Death and Dying*. For the sake of brevity, some of them are outlined below.

Basic Stages of Grief
Shock
Emotional dysfunction
Depression and loneliness
Physical symptoms
A sense of guilt
Anger or rage
Difficulty or inability to return to usual activities
Gradual adjustment to your "altered" life

Acceptance of your "altered" life

Shock: Whether a death is expected or sudden, shock is often a first reaction. You cannot believe or imagine that the individual has died.

Emotional dysfunction: Grief has a way of affecting your core personality. Your personality may experience temporal changes. For example, where you used to be calm and docile, you may become hyper and snappy or worse.

Depression and loneliness: These two are grouped together because they often go hand-in-hand. This duo may be the most dangerous of all. Depression is a very serious symptom and must be monitored closely. Depression results from feelings of hopelessness. You feel as if your situation will never change. Depression often promotes thoughts and feelings of loneliness and abandonment. If you are depressed or you sense that someone you love is depressed, please seek professional help.

Physical symptoms: Researchers suggest that 80% or more of all illnesses are virtually stress based or preventable. That means *you* may be making yourself sick. Headaches, ulcers, hair loss, weight loss, weight gain, dehydration and anxiety attacks often accompany those who are grieving. Chemical imbalances may also occur.

Guilt: Guilt often occurs on two different extremes especially when it involves someone elderly or an unexpected, sudden loss. Many people feel they could have or should have done more for the deceased. Some even feel they were negligent in some way and could have prevented the death. If you are facing guilt, realize and accept that you cannot change the past, and learn from any mistakes you feel you have made. You must forgive yourself. We will discuss forgiveness in greater detail as we proceed.

About Life-Support Decisions

In our technological society, many people are faced with decisions concerning whether or not to initiate or terminate life support. Do not *second guess* your decision if you made the choice to initiate or terminate life support, or both. Generally speaking, all life support decisions come with a recommendation or analysis from trained medical personnel. Rarely is the decision based on a whim or for unethical reasons. After careful consideration and based on the information you received, you made an informed decision. Know that you made the best decision at the time. Do not allow guilt to consume you. While this is often easier said than done, choose not to dwell on the decision. Dwell instead on their life. Remember when they were strong, vibrant and healthy.

Anger or rage: Anger is very common. Sometimes it is anger towards the deceased because they left you, or it may be anger at those around you. You may feel parents, siblings or children could have or should have done more or treated the deceased better. Maybe you were the only one in the family who seemed concerned or attempted to do anything. Maybe you were the only person on the job who donated money for flowers. You may be angry because the workload now falls on you. There are many reasons one may be angry. If you recognize that you are angry, get help before you make matters worse. Unresolved anger has a tendency to cause people to do and / or say things they regret.

Difficulty returning to normal activities: Many people feel they *just cannot go on* with life as they once knew it. Some take long leaves of absence from their jobs or even quit. Others abandon relationships they have had for years. For some, even simple tasks like housework or a trip to the grocery store seems insurmountable. Sometimes people feel that they are dishonoring the deceased if they *enjoy* life again without them.

Gradual adjustment to your altered life: You begin to adjust to the reality that your life will be changed forever. You will gradually participate in prior activities and become more comfortable being around the people, places and things of the past. You can move forward despite your pain.

Acceptance of your altered life: You realize *and* accept that you have suffered a significant loss. You make a quality decision to continue to lead a productive and healthy life. Acceptance does not mean you like what happened. It simply means you have chosen to function as best you can now that your loved one is gone.

In addition to the above stages, many people face fear. These fears include:

Fear of the future.
Fear of being alone.
Fear of making decisions.
Fear of change.
Fear of not knowing what to do next or how to do it.
Fear that another loved one will die.

Do not allow fear to dominate your thoughts or your life. Fear will keep you from moving forward, and sometimes keep you from moving at all. If you allow it to, fear will paralyze or cripple you emotionally.

"My dad just had a heart attack."
One of my girlfriends in High School had two of the best parents imaginable. They were inseparable and very kind and considerate towards one another. I always enjoyed being around them because they held each other in such high esteem. You knew it was genuine and not just an act for company. Not only

did they treat each other well, they made me feel like part of the family. It was always a great atmosphere in their home.

I almost went into panic mode when my girlfriend called one day, *"My dad just had a heart attack. He collapsed at work and they are taking him to emergency."* She went on to say, *"I can deal with machines and tubes everywhere, but he just can't be dead."* Being an only child, she was daddy's little girl. Her father was always so good to her and he was very proud of his baby. All her life he has been her Rock of Gibraltar and her pillar of strength. Anytime she needed or wanted anything, she went to her father. Now, he was fighting for his life. She tried to keep herself together, but for the first time in her own life, her world was shaken. When she arrived at the hospital, there were indeed machines and tubes everywhere, but it was too late. She received the worst news imaginable, *"He is dead."*

Honestly, I did not think of my friend losing her father; all I could really think of was her mother. Her parents had been married for over 30 years and when I say her mother depended on him for everything, I mean EVERYTHING. He loved and pampered her like Prince Charming in a made for television movie. They lived such a beautiful real life love story. I remember thinking, "How in the world will she ever be able to live without him?" As fast as I could I drove from college straight to their home, about a 90 minute drive. It was filled with friends and relatives, most of whom I did not know. I tried to be polite to everyone but I had only one goal in mind: to get to her mother. At first I couldn't find her. Finally, I asked someone and was told, *"She is over there."* As I looked toward where they pointed, I saw her on the floor, balled up in the corner, staring into space. She was just sitting there, propped up against the wall. It angered me that no one was with her. She was all alone. People would just walk by looking at her, shaking their head in pity. I went over to her, kneeled down on the floor beside her and just held her. After what seemed to be an eternity, she finally acknowledged me and embraced me. We probably stayed in that position for an hour in dead silence only interrupted by an occasional voice saying, *"There she is."*

Through all the planning for the memorial services, as well as the actual service, I stuck to her like glue. She was unable to do it alone. For the first few days after her husband passed, she just cried. When she wasn't crying, she sat in silence. Her relatives would often tell her she needed to, *"Get yourself together,"* to which I was ready to tell them a thing or two, but I didn't. Every day I went and simply embraced her or just held her hand. I rarely said anything to her unless she asked for my input. My presence was all she needed to bring comfort. She was so afraid of her future without him. She felt totally inadequate without him. For a period of time, she refused to face the thought of life without him. Fortunately, with the support of family and friends, she was able to finally get through her grieving process and is once again bringing comfort and encouragement to others. She was able to conquer her fears of living without her beloved mate.

How to Break Free From Fear

This is a brief quick start guide with three steps to get you started on the path of your journey to freedom. For detailed information on overcoming your fears, please check out the many online and bookstore resources that are available on this subject. For easier recall, I have labeled them the Triple A's. If you follow these simple steps, you will be well on your way.

The Triple A's to break free from fear

Acknowledge. You must acknowledge or admit *what* you are afraid of. Once you acknowledge your fear(s), you will be in a better position to overcome it. If you deny the existence of your fear, you will not be able to conquer it. The first step to getting help is to acknowledge the areas of struggle or fear. For example, if you are afraid of flying, admit it. If you fear change, admit it. If you are afraid of the dark, acknowledge it.

Analyze. Ask yourself why you are afraid. Are you afraid to be home alone? If so, why? Are you afraid of making financial decisions? If so, why? Have you invested money and lost it? Are you afraid to be around people? If so, why? Did something happen to you as a result of being in a crowd? Are you afraid of the dark? If so, why are you afraid? Ask yourself, *"Am I afraid for no reason?"* Determine whether your fears are founded in tangible facts or experiences, or if they are runaway emotions.

Attack. You must find a way to attack and conquer your fear(s). Depending on what you are afraid of, you may want someone to help you. As in the earlier example, if you are afraid of flying, book a short flight one way. Take someone with you, if necessary. Somehow, someway, find a way to attack and face your fear.

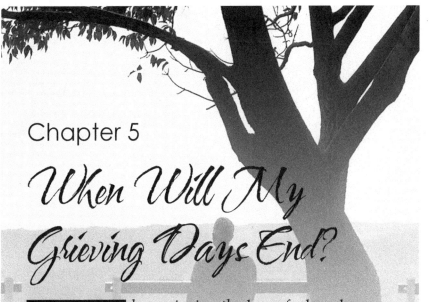

Chapter 5

When Will My Grieving Days End?

When grieving the loss of a loved one, you may ask, "When will my grieving days end?" "Will the pain ever subside?" The answers to these questions depend on a number of variables including your belief system, religious background, age, life experiences and the type of loss you have suffered. All these factors play a part in the grieving process.

There is no timetable for grief. There is no three step plan and suddenly, grieving is over. Your grieving period will last as long as it takes for you to adjust to the multiple changes that occur after your loss. In fact, the more significant the relationship with your loved one, the more potential impact their absence may have upon you. This resource provides numerous tools to help you through the grieving process.

If you apply the principles outlined, your adjustment time will be shortened and less painful. Keep in mind the loss you have suffered is significant. You will never forget your loved one, but you can and must adjust to life with their memory in your heart.

Chapter 6

Grief Must Be Managed, Monitored, & Measured

Grief must be managed. *Manage* means to *exert control over; to make submissive to one's authority; to direct or control the use of.* You must manage or control grief. If you allow pain and anguish to run rampant, your days of being functional are over. Regardless of how you feel, you must begin the process of managing your grief. This can be done in a number of different ways. You may need to seek professional help or talk to your priest or minister. You must do something and start somewhere. Grief will not go away on its own. You have to drive it away from you.

He was only 18.

One of my music industry friends often traveled out of town for business, and I usually helped him book and purchase his tickets. He called one day and said he needed to change his flight arrangements to attend a funeral. After giving my condolences, I made the ticket changes and then asked him what happened. The son of one of his colleagues was killed in a car accident; he was only 18. It turns out that his parents bought him a brand new car for Christmas, and in less than 30 days, he was killed in the very gift they gave him. You can imagine the pain and anguish his parents felt; not to mention the many thoughts and regrets they had. "If only we hadn't bought him the car." "If only we had driven him ourselves." "If only we told him to stay home." The truth is, those things may or may not have changed anything. Every teenager wants their own car. Generally speaking, it is every parent's dream to give their children the desires of their heart. Is it wrong to give teenagers cars? Of course not, but you can believe if parents in these types of circumstances do not manage their feelings of guilt and grief, everything around them will crumble, including their marriage.

After the sudden death of a child, many marital relationships suffer. For those that survive, there is often unavoidable friction. One main reason is because inwardly, one spouse blames the other spouse for the tragedy. Neither party may be at fault, but that does not keep one of them from silently (or loudly) being blamed. They may never come out and say the words "it's your fault," but deep down inside, they feel the spouse could have done something to prevent death. I call this the SAF syndrome. SAF stands for Silently at Fault. It's not verbalized, but it is there nonetheless.

Another reason may be one spouse feels they just cannot go on with life or business as usual without their child. In either case, both spouses must make a decision to help each other adjust to the loss, and not take their hurt and pain out on each other.

Communication between the spouses is critical, especially in times like these. What if in the above situation one spouse did not want the son to have a car in the first place? Imagine the stress and strain that would put on the relationship. They would certainly blame the spouse whether silently or not.

Grief Must Be Monitored

Monitor means *to check; to track; to keep watch over; to check systematically or scrutinize.* You must keep a pulse on grief and be aware of it at all times. It can sneak up on you at times you least expect. Recognize when grief *hits* you. Consider keeping a journal. Journaling often helps to release stress and, oftentimes, it is easier to write down your feelings and thoughts than it is to talk about them. You can be brutally honest with yourself and express how you really feel. What you write will be for your eyes only unless you choose to share what you have written. You may recognize a pattern which will be very beneficial in helping you through the grieving process.

"Practicing what I preach."

As I was "practicing what I preach" by keeping my emotions and grief in *check*, one day I needed to buy a birthday card for my beloved sister. So, I went to the Hallmark store. Only the best for her will do.

There were so many beautiful cards and trinkets everywhere. As I walked down the aisle towards the birthday cards, I noticed a *"Happy Birthday Mother"* card. It seemed to stand ten feet tall. All of a sudden I just froze in place. I couldn't move. I tried, but nothing doing. To make matters worse, it was as if someone turned on a water facet. Tears began to run down my face faster than I could stop them. It was uncontrollable. I couldn't even reach for a tissue. I was just frozen. I did my best not to be noticed which was extremely difficult. I knew if someone asked me, *"What's wrong?"*, that would increase the water pressure. I stayed facing the cards and avoided eye contact with anyone.

Once I was finally able to go from a steady stream of tears to a slow leak, and able to move again, I got out of that store as quickly as I could. I was shocked. Not because I was crying (which, by the way, is okay), but because I had come to the store to buy cards before and did not break down crying. Needless to say, I stayed away from the card store for a while and unfortunately, that year, my sister did not receive a beautiful birthday card. I'm happy to report I am once again able to shop at Hallmark which is one of my favorite stores.

"Those dreaded Mother's Days."
My maternal grandmother died when I was in

college. As a young child, I witnessed the beautiful relationship between my mother and my grandmother. If there was a definition in the dictionary of how a mother and daughter should treat and love each other, my mother's and grandmother's pictures would be next to it. My mother cherished her mother twenty-four hours a day, seven days a week.

The only time I ever saw or heard my mother cry was when my grandmother died. Before then, she was never sad. Anytime she would attend a funeral, she told me, "No matter who is in the casket, I always see my mother." Wow, how tragic that was. What an image to have constantly. Repeatedly seeing someone you love in a casket. Unfortunately, she did not know she could manage and monitor her grief. At that time, neither did I.

For years I dreaded Mother's Day because that day made mother so sad. My sister and I always went to church with my mother on Mother's Day. Every time the Pastor would say "Happy Mother's Day to all the mothers," my mother would just cry; many times, out loud.

Words cannot express how helpless I felt. It was heart wrenching. Parents console the children. *They* make everything alright. *They* make things better. It's not supposed to be the other way around. How do you console Mama? Mama is the one with all the wisdom. Mama has all the answers. I didn't know what to do or what to say. Fortunately, many years later, a Mother's Day finally came when she did not cry hearing the words, "Happy Mother's Day."

Author's Note

If you know of someone who has lost a mother, father, grandmother, grandfather or child, consider being their *adoptive* parent or child. You are in no way attempting to replace their loved one, but you can help fill a huge void in their life and help them adjust to life with this great loss. You can share life's moments with them, as well as be there when they need a listening ear or a shoulder to cry on. Over time, you will forge a beautiful relationship and help someone through one of the most traumatic losses one could ever experience. If you have lost your mother, father, grandmother, grandfather or child, please consider reaching out to someone else who has felt the same pain.

Grief must be measured

Measured is *the degree or extent of something; to mark; to limit; a basis of comparison.* You must measure grief. What does it mean to measure grief you might ask? You must locate where you are in the grieving process. Are you moving through the stages of grief or are you stuck in a rut and can't seem to move forward? In other words, are you able to continue or begin functioning as you did prior to your loss? Have you returned to work and able to focus on your assignments? Are you driving yourself again? What about household chores and tasks inside and outside?

Are you again able to complete them, or have you lost all motivation? Are you able to think clearly and make good decisions? These types of questions help to measure grief, allowing you to determine if you are progressing through the stages or not. Once that is determined, you can begin to lessen the affects of grief on your life. Acknowledge where you are and proceed from there.

"They all died in the fire."

When someone asked, *"Isn't it sad about those children killed in the fire?"*, at the time, I hadn't heard about it. As a grandmother babysat three of her young grandchildren overnight, somehow, the space heater caught fire as did the entire house. All attempts to rescue the grandmother and children were unsuccessful. They all died in the fire.

To my dismay, one of the mothers of the children was someone I knew personally. You cannot imagine the pain and anguish suffered by the mothers of the children. Not only that, the grandmother died, which means they lost their child and their mother at the same time. How painful.

The reason I share this account is because the children had requested to spend that night at one of the aunt's houses. She told them, *"Not tonight. You can come over in the morning."* Needless to say, "morning" never came.

I decided to go to the funeral service and support the family I was acquainted with. At that time, I had never attended the funeral of a child or anyone else killed in a fire, but even if I had, it would not have prepared me for what was to come. When I arrived at the church and entered the sanctuary, there were four open caskets with three children and one adult. Nobody mentioned that the funeral for all four would take place at the same time. I thought I would see one casket with one child, instead, there were four. It was heart wrenching to say the least. Every one was longing for their son, their daughter, their mother, their grandmother, their sibling, their niece, their nephew and countless other relationships, all at the same time. It is something you never want to experience.

You can be sure the aunt has had to overcome many challenges as she copes with the loss of her mother as well as her niece and nephews. Does she blame herself? If she had allowed them to spend the night, would they still be alive? In addition to those feelings and questions, do the siblings blame her for the death of their mother and children? Every one must measure their grief. Whatever your cause of grief, get rid of the guilt. Stop the "what if?" Stop the "if only", and locate where you are. Once you have located yourself, get the help you need. How is this family surviving? One day at a time.

"He just needed to get away from the situation."

A young couple with two small children had a huge argument one day and the husband got in his car and left the premises. He said he just "needed to get away from the situation." A few hours later, the wife received the news that her husband had been killed in a car accident. Needless to say, the wife was devastated. For years she blamed herself for his death. Although he was not the at fault driver, she could not forgive herself for what she considered *her part* in his death. Fortunately, she was supported by people who were able to help her through those feelings. It was a long, hard road to recovery, but she recovered.

For those of you who are married, and have been married for a number of years, you know it takes time to work through the lumps and bumps a marriage can bring. That is especially true in the early years of marriage; two different people, from two different worlds, trying to get on the same page. It can be difficult. By managing, monitoring, and measuring your grief, you can grieve fully without escalating any negative effects unnecessarily.

Personal Notes

_____

_____

_____

_____

_____

_____

_____

_____

_____

_____

_____

Personal Notes

_____

_____

_____

_____

_____

_____

_____

_____

_____

_____

_____

Personal Notes

_____

_____

_____

_____

_____

_____

_____

_____

_____

_____

_____

_____

Part 3
Grief
Recovery

Chapter 7

I'm Drowning! Help Me!

Words are very powerful and important. Have you ever heard of the self-fulfilling prophecy? Sociologist Robert K. Merton coined the phrase and the theory behind it. Basically it says that if you say or hear something long enough, you will eventually believe it. Whether it's true or not; whether it's positive or negative you will own it as truth. If you speak positively about your grieving process, the day will come when you will actually be better today, than you were yesterday.

Begin helping yourself by starting each day with encouraging words. When you wake up and even throughout each day, say something like: *"Today, I am one day closer to my healing. Today, I will be better than I was yesterday."*

Helping Yourself

The following helps are very practical and simple,

yet extremely effective, if you apply them. Though this list is in no way exhaustive, you must decide to do many of them on your own; others will require support and assistance. Hopefully from the previous information, you have been able to locate where you are in the grieving process. There is a worksheet (Appendix B) provided at the end of this book to help you identify the areas you may need to focus on.

Acknowledgement. Acknowledge your feelings of pain, anger, hurt etc. It is the first step towards healing. Once you are able to recognize where you are emotionally, you will be able to determine where you are in the grieving process. From there, you will be able to get any help you may need.

Talk it out. It is okay to express your feelings. Tell someone or everyone how you are feeling. They may not understand all the emotions you are facing, but it will be a great release for you to talk it out. This is not a license to unleash all your anger and frustration. It simply means you find someone(s) you are comfortable with and get things "off your chest."

Listen. Help is everywhere if you will be open to it. Chances are there are people surrounding you that can offer good advice and emotional support. They may have experienced a significant loss as well, and may be able to offer insight for the days and years to come.

You are on already traveled ground. Allow the wisdom of others to help you. In doing so, you may avoid many of the pitfalls and missteps that can happen during this time. The lessons others have learned will benefit you, if not now, in the future. Someone once said, "Be as smart as a cow. A cow eats the hay and spits out the sticks." What does that mean? It means to receive and apply the good, useful and helpful advice, and throw away the rest.

Do not try to go it alone. If you are fortunate enough to have people in your life who care about you, let them help you through the process. Allow the "village" to assist you as you heal from your loss. The English poet John Donne said, *"No man is an island entire of itself; every man is a piece of the continent, a part of the main…"* We need one another, especially during times of loss. Let others help you!

Be careful making important decisions. Take your time making important decisions. During this period of time of grief you may not be thinking as clearly. You are dealing with various issues and emotions. You do not want to make an emotional decision that you may regret later. For any important decisions that must be made, do your due diligence.

If possible, have someone you trust who has the expertise, review your decision before it is final. They should be able to help you make a good, quality decision. For any decisions that can wait, let them wait.

Focus your energy on successfully navigating life after loss. The time will come when you will be more emotionally grounded and better able to make necessary decisions.

   Do not be in denial. Do not act as if you have not suffered a significant loss. Denial will only make the healing process longer. As mentioned in the section on *How to Break Free from Fear,* acknowledgement is critical for the healing process to begin. For example, if your spouse has died, start by saying something like, *"My beautiful husband/wife has died. I love and miss them so much. I'm glad for the years we spent together."* This may be simple for some, but it is very difficult for others. Whether acknowledgment of your loss is easy or difficult, it must be done. Do it today.

Take care of your body

- **Rest your body.** When you are physically exhausted it affects everything; how you think, how you feel, how you react and what you say. Sleep is important for concentration, memory formation and the repair of damage to your body's cells during the day. Although you are experiencing many emotions, try to quiet your mind (thoughts). It will be difficult to rest if your mind is racing every minute of the day. Try your best to sleep.

- **Drink water.** Water plays a role in almost every bodily function. It regulates the temperature of the body; carries nutrients and oxygen to cells; protects organs and tissues; cushions joints and removes toxins. If you become dehydrated in the process, it will only make things worse.

- **Eat.** Your body needs the nourishment to stay healthy. There is literature everywhere to help you begin or maintain a healthy diet. Try your best not to binge or allow your emotions to drive your eating habits or food choices. Make sure you eat healthy foods in healthy amounts.

   Surround yourself with positive people. Stay away from people who are negative. If they call, let the answering machine take a message. If they visit, change the subject. If you are uncomfortable with either of those options, consider asking a friend or relative to speak with them. Have them explain that if they are going to speak to you, they must leave all the drama and negativity behind. Negative people speak negative words, think negative thoughts and are usually unhappy and depressed. You don't need someone telling you how bad it is or asking you, *"How are you going to make it?"* You will have enough thoughts, feelings and questions like those of your own. This is a time when you need encouragement and reassurance. Surround yourself with positive people who will help keep you afloat emotionally, not pull you down into more grief, sorrow and sadness.

Set up a support system. Ask those you love and trust to check on you daily or weekly. It is quite comforting to know you are not alone and others care about you. A simple telephone call or a personal visit will go a long way in the healing process. With all the advance computer and mobile technologies, communicating and connecting with others is one of the easiest things you can do. There are Skype, face time, video conferencing, instant messaging, email and so much more.

Use a journal. Many times it is easier to write down your feelings than to express them verbally. As stated previously, journaling is a great way to not only relieve stress, but also helps you identity where you are in the grieving process. The journal will be for your eyes only unless you choose to share it.

Get out of the house. A change of venue will go a long way to improve your emotional state of mind. The change in scenery will be beneficial. Call a neighbor, a relative or a friend to drive you somewhere or take a walk with you. You can go to a restaurant or just sit on the porch or deck.

Read your condolences. When you are going through the motions of planning and attending services, you are not really focused on anything. Many times you do not remember details or faces. As you read the testimonials of the love, honor and respect individuals have for you or your loved one, you will be inspired and encouraged. Review your condolences often. This is sure to help bring healing.

Do not isolate yourself. Don't push away people who are attempting to help. Two are better than one, and in the multitude of counselors, there is safety. While there is always a chance you will run across people who are not genuine, for the most part, people are sincere and can help you if you let them.

Help and encourage someone else. Do you remember *"the Golden Rule?"* Do unto others as you would have them do unto you. Find a way to help someone else who is hurting. You may have to really push yourself to do this, but you need to do it. A brief telephone call to someone who has lost a loved one is a great place to start. If you know someone who is ill, consider sending a Get Well card or flowers. There are also numerous volunteer opportunities available in hospitals, nursing homes, schools, libraries, day care centers and religious institutions to name a few. Find a volunteer area you enjoy and commit to helping a few hours a week. As you turn your attention toward helping someone else, you will be surprised how much better you will feel.

Join a support group. Many local communities, as well as churches and parishes, have support groups. Joining one will remind you that you are not alone, and can offer additional help and resources. There are many different support groups. There are those for women only and men only. There are groups for widows and widowers. They have support groups for people with children and those without children. There are also groups from youth and teenagers to senior citizens. To find a group in your area, go to www.google.com. In the search type in support groups and your city and state. You will find numerous resources to assist you with locating a group best suited for your needs.

Acceptance of your altered life. Realize *and* accept that you have suffered a significant loss. Make a quality decision to continue to lead a productive and healthy life.

Gradually Adjust. Adjust to the reality that your life has been changed forever. As you become more comfortable being around the people, places and things of the past, gradually participate in prior activities. It may be difficult and unnerving initially because your loved one is not with you, but keep going. Take one step at a time, one day at a time. Rest assured there are brighter days ahead.

Talk to your Priest, Pastor or Professional Counselor. If you are really struggling, seek professional help. There is no shame in seeking help. The shame is knowing you need help and not seeking it.

Obstacles to Grieving

*"To spare oneself from grief at all cost can be
achieved only at the price of total detachment, which
excludes the ability to experience happiness."*
Erich Fromm

As we continue to focus on how you can help
yourself, it is important to briefly mention that certain
conditions, events, and circumstances can be obstacles
to grieving. These may include:

- *Living in our fast-paced society.* The need to
  return to work or school soon after a significant loss, many times rushes a person through
  the grieving process.

- *Having no formal way to express grief.* This
  may happen, for example, after a miscarriage
  or abortion. With other losses there is usually a
  burial or memorial ceremony which allows the
  parents the opportunity to express their grief
  and obtain a sense of closure. This is generally not the case with regards to miscarriage or
  abortion.

- *Being unable to participate in a burial or memorial ceremony.* Sometimes you cannot participate in burial or memorial services to express grief. Maybe you do not live near where

services are being held; or for some reason or another, you are unable to attend memorial services. This may make it difficult to receive closure or to begin the grieving process.

• *Having certain psychological or cognitive disorders.* Conditions such as depression, high anxiety or other mental disorders, intellectual disability, or substance abuse can interfere with a person's ability to grieve.

There is a man whose wife recently passed. They had two children, one diagnosed with autism. When the father told his autistic child that his mother had died, the child asked,
　　"Where is she?"
　　"She's in heaven" the father responded.
　　"Okay" replied the child. Every now and then, the child will say to his father,
　　"Mom is in heaven, right?"
　　"Yes, she is."
　　"Okay."

Another major obstacle that must be addressed is unforgiveness. In order to successfully move through the pain of a significant loss, you simply must forgive. As explained in detail below, not only must you forgive yourself, you must also forgive others.

• *Forgive yourself.* Do not pitch your tent or

park your camper on the campgrounds of self-pity. If you have any feelings of guilt, forgive yourself. You should not and cannot afford to focus on negative words that were said, or irritating deeds that were done. You cannot change yesterday; IT IS GONE. You can, TO-DAY, make a decision to forgive yourself and focus on the positive regardless of how massive or minute. When you look back over your life, there will always be areas or mistakes you wish you could banish forever. You can't. The past is the past. Retrospect is just that–retrospect. Going forward, you can make a decision to carefully consider your ways so that you can live regret free.

• **Forgive others.** If you believe you have been mistreated, you must forgive the person(s) who wronged you. Even though you are grieving the loss of a loved one, you may have unforgiveness towards the deceased or someone else for something they have done, or should have done. You must forgive them. The common denominator of unforgiveness is generally broken trust or betrayal. You trusted someone to provide or protect or conceal or support you in some way, and they did not. They betrayed you. As a result, it caused great pain and anguish.

Maybe you were victim of a horrible crime like incest or rape. Maybe you were abandoned or mistreated by family. Maybe someone caused you to lose your job, committed fraud or stole something valuable from you. As difficult as it may be, **you must forgive them**. Please understand this vital point: **forgiveness is not for the offender; it is for you.**

A *University of Tennessee* study exploring the effect of a forgiving personality on both psychological and physical stress responses, suggests that harboring feelings of betrayal may be linked to high blood pressure which can ultimately lead to stroke, kidney or heart failure, or even death. Forgiveness may be a matter of life and death. In addition to potential health issues, when you hold on to the hurt and pain of an offense, you give the offenders too much power and control over your life. If you do not forgive:

> *Offenders control your thoughts.* You are continually reminded of and bombarded with the thought(s) of what they did to you. That keeps you on an emotional roller coaster. You cannot progress because you are constantly being pulled in a negative direction. They are with you at all times, just not physically. However, they are emotionally attached to you.

> *Offenders control where you go or don't go.* They control your movements. There are places you will not go because you do not want to risk run-

ning into those you have not forgiven. When you allow offenders to control your movements, they are also dictating your life. Do you really want someone who has offended you to have that much influence over your life?

Offenders control what you do. There are events, especially family gatherings or work related functions that you will not attend because you know he or she or they will be there. What a shame. You are the favorite cousin, but you will not attend the family reunion because you cannot forgive.

Offenders control who you associate with. You disconnect with people simply because they are associated with someone you are avoiding.

The above are very basic examples of what generally happens when you harbor unforgiveness. Be honest with yourself. In light of the information presented, look around to see if there is anyone you have not forgiven. You will not go through life without having multiple opportunities to be hurt and offended. Sometimes hurts are deliberate, but oftentimes they are accidental. Regardless of the reason you were hurt or offended, you must forgive. A few more points to mention:

- Forgiveness is not based on whether or not the person deserves to be forgiven.

- Forgiveness does not mean you forget about the pain and suffering they caused and continue to put yourself in harms way.

- Forgiveness does not mean you have to be their best friend.

- Forgiveness is not connected to whether or not they care if you forgive them. They may be callous towards you. That is irrelevant. Remember, forgiveness is for YOU.

Here is a good measure for whether you have forgiven someone or not: can you see them, hear their name or think of them and not want to pay them back or see them suffer in some way for what they did to you or someone you care about? If you cannot, then you know you have some work to do in this area. Depending on the severity of the offense, you may not be able to do it on your own. If you are really struggling with the inability to forgive, please seek professional help.

Give yourself time to heal. This is a process. Healing may not happen overnight. The definition of process is to *begin and carry on a series of actions or measures.* It means *to pass from one stage to another.* It also means *to make progress or to advance.* Apply the principles of healing and allow time for them to work. Remember to take one day at a time. With the right support system, the day will come when you will not only feel better, you will be better.

Are you "Ultra Sensitive?" It is understandable
that you are going through a very difficult time. You
are faced with feelings, decisions and changes you
may not be prepared for. As a result, it is very likely
you will become more emotionally sensitive than
usual. When you are grieving, it is very common to
be easily offended by the words or actions of others.
You may misinterpret something that is said or done.
You may feel those around you are insensitive and
"just don't understand." That may be true. However,
especially during this time period, remember it is an
adjustment for EVERYONE. Although you may have
suffered the greatest loss, keep in mind that others are
impacted as well. Be patient with those around you.

Keep Your Loved One's Memory Alive
Recalling fond memories is very beneficial when being healed from grief. If at all possible, find a way to
keep alive the life, memory and legacy of your loved
one. Do not try to act as if they never lived. Celebrate
their life. Do not be in denial. Deliberately remember
them.

"I'm sorry I won't see any of your children."
I will never forget when my best girlfriend's
mother was ill. Actually, she was dying. I am not sure
if the family knew she was dying, but I didn't. Her
mother was always so spunky and full of life. She

never left home without being well dressed and looking sharp. I really loved her.

At the time she passed, my girlfriend was almost nine months pregnant with her first child. You know how it is when you are expecting and looking forward to your "bundle of joy." She was so excited. On the one hand, she was so happy, but on the other hand she was saddened because her mother was sick.

I will never forget the words her mother spoke to her, "Baby, I'm sorry I won't be here to see any of your children." How that broke my heart. No girl wants to have a baby without mama; especially the first one. I didn't cry in front of my girlfriend then, but every time I thought about what her mother said to her, I cried.

In spite of the pain she felt with losing her mother, she made a decision to make sure her children knew their grandmother. She now has two beautiful, well adjusted children. They know quite a bit about their maternal grandmother, even though she died before they were born. She keeps her mother's memory alive with her children through pictures, stories and many fond memories.

Below are a few practical suggestions on how to keep your loved ones memory alive.

1. Make a donation in their name to their favorite charity.

2. Make a point to keep in touch with the people they kept in touch with.

3. Start some type of memorial fund.

4. Start a scholarship in their name.

5. Donate their clothing to needy individuals.

6. Make a donation in their name to their alma mater.

7. Send an "in memory of" card to relatives and friends. Send it on their birthday or some other date of your choosing.

8. Ask family, friends, neighbors and co-workers to write a special memory of them. You can then compile a scrapbook.

9. Research/create your family tree. Make it a group project for the entire family.

10. Make a decision to remember the good and

positive things they did.

Before we move forward, let's review the ways you can help yourself through this process:

- Acknowledge your feelings
- Talk it out
- Listen to others
- Do not try to go it alone
- Be careful making important decisions
- Do not be in denial
- Take care of your body
- Surround yourself with positive people
- Set up a personal support system
- Use a journal
- Get out of the house
- Read your condolences
- Do not isolate yourself
- Help and encourage someone else
- Join a support group
- Accept your altered life
- Gradually adjust to your altered life
- Talk to your Priest, Pastor or a Professional Counselor
- Remember the obstacles to grieving
- Give yourself time to heal
- Keep your loved one's memory alive

As this portion concludes, it is our hope that you received enough information from the previous chapters to move forward in the grieving process. As we turn our attention to helping others, we pray that you have personally been helped and encouraged. Refer to this information often. You will not retain or grasp everything in one or two readings. Allow enough time and apply what you have learned. Rest assured you can make it through this very difficult time. However, in order to make it through, you must make a decision to do so. As you apply these principles, continue to take one day at a time. In time, with faith and patience, your joy will return, your peace of mind will return and your heart will heal.

Chapter 8

Practical Ways to Help Someone Who is Grieving

s you position yourself to help someone who is grieving, keep in mind this is a very sensitive time in their life. They are faced with decisions, feelings and emotions for which they may not be prepared. Your role is to help and support them. You may feel totally inadequate, uncomfortable and awkward. However, rest assured you can make a difference.

It goes without saying that many of you may not be trained grief counselors. However, the day will come when you need to provide comfort to someone else. Review this material often. In doing so, you will be better equipped to help someone who may be grieving.

Remember the Survivor(s)

Sometimes relationships die with the death of a loved one, too. Often the survivor loses the companionship and friendship of others who were associated with the deceased. Make a point to keep in touch with the surviving individual(s). If you called and/or visited them in the past, continue to do so. Where appropriate, if you shared special activities continue inviting them to participate again. They may decide not to join you, but still make the offer.

When someone is grieving, that is not the time to psychoanalyze their every thought, word or deed. Position yourself to assist them. When they cry, offer tissue and a shoulder. People who are grieving need encouragement, support and reassurance. Keep in mind, that life as they have known it, will be changed forever. Because of their significant loss, everything in their life must be reconfigured. Your support, patience and understanding will go a long way in helping them through the grieving process.

Practical Ways to Help Someone Who is Grieving

The following information will assist you in helping someone who is grieving. Again, this list is in no way exhaustive, but these tools will help get you started.

Be a good listener. Shhhh! Don't do all the talking. When people are grieving, many times no feedback is wanted or needed. They just want a listening ear. Allow them to talk without interruption.

Once they express themselves, then you can interject. If you feel something they said needs correcting, don't judge them. Wait on an appropriate moment and gently give your perspective.

Let them talk about their loved one. Generally speaking, the grieving individual is longing to reminisce about them. They want to share a story, or hear something encouraging about them. Too often, because it is uncomfortable or awkward, others avoid mentioning or discussing anything about the deceased. If they want to talk about their loved one, allow them to.

Watch what you say. Remember, this is a very sensitive time period. Awkward and uncomfortable feelings often cause those desiring to be a source of comfort to feel helpless to ease their sorrow. Sometimes you do not have to say anything. A hug or gentle squeeze will go a long way. People are well-meaning, but oftentimes in these situations, they say the wrong things. Whatever you say, make sure it is encouraging and not depressing. In addition, stay away from phrases like: *"I know how you feel"*, *"God knows best"*, *"Don't cry"* and *"You have to move on."* Those statements may make them angry. Examples of things you might say:

- I am sorry for your loss.
- I really don't know what to say right now, but please know I am available to help you anyway I can.
- You and your family will be in my thoughts and

prayers.

- We all need help at times like these; I am here to help you.
- Anytime you want to talk, whether early in the morning or late at night, do not hesitate to call. I will make myself available.
- I will continue to pray for you.
- You have my condolences.

Whatever you see needs to be done, do it. Some things need permission, others will not. Some items require money, some do not. If the floor needs sweeping, get the broom and just start sweeping. Instead of saying, "If there is anything I can do, let me know," be specific in your offer of assistance.

Tony Cooke, in his book, *Life after Death*, explains how it is better to make specific offers of help as opposed to general offers. Below are a few examples he cites. Notice the pattern of offering specific help.

- "May I help you with calling friends and family members?"
- "Why don't we sit down together and make a list of what needs to be done?"
- "I'd like to bring dinner over this evening. May I?"
- "Would you like me to pick up incoming family members from the airport?"
- "May I help you with your children over the next few days?"

- "Would you like me to drive you to the funeral home and be with you while you make arrangements?"

Consider the following list of things that often need to be done after the loss of a loved one that grieving friends do not think to ask about.

- Buy stamps
- Purchase groceries
- Clean the house
- Wash linens
- Empty trash receptacles
- Rake the leaves
- Mow the lawn
- Plant flowers
- Shovel the snow
- Prepare/provide meals
- Offer to provide transportation
- Make phone calls
- Baby-sit
- House-sit
- Pet-sit
- Pay phone bill
- Wash car(s)
- Put Gasoline in car(s)
- Purchase paper goods
- Purchase toiletries
- Purchase garbage bags
- Address thank you cards

Visit them. Please visit them if possible. Seeing a friendly face will really help them emotionally. Your visit will give them something else to think on and talk about as they are left to reorder their life. Simply reading with them, watching television with them or joining them in an activity will go a long way.

Call them. Take the time to call. Again, to hear a friendly voice is a great diversion from their new routine without their loved one. Keep your conversation brief, unless they desire to talk longer. Keep your conversation positive and uplifting. As previously stated, with all the latest technology, communicating with someone is easy.

Pray for them. Please remember them in your prayers. Your prayers for them will continue to work 24 hours a day, 7 days a week and 365 days a year. Whether they are near or far, pray that they have peace and be comforted. Even if they do not understand or believe in the power of prayer, you know prayer won't hurt them.

Send a card or personal note. There is nothing like a card, personal letter or note. When someone receives something personal just for them, it really makes them feel thought of and special. To know that someone took the time to write something specific is very encouraging. If you purchase a ready made greeting card, take a moment to write a personal note

to them. They will be able to read it as often as they
like and for years to come.

Offer to take them somewhere. Help them get out
of the house. A change of scenery will help improve
their emotional state of mind. If you know places they
enjoy, take them there. Even if you simply drive or
walk by without going inside, that will be beneficial.

Ask them how you can help. There will be things
they need that you are unaware of, especially family members. Many times family members and close
friends feel they know what is needed or wanted.
This may be true, but ask them anyway. Caution: do
not make promises to them you cannot keep. Only
agree to those things you can follow through on.

Be a person they can trust. Be trustworthy. If they
confide in you, do not gossip or tell others what they
shared. They opened their heart to you because they
believed it was safe to do so. They have enough emotions to manage without feeling that their confidence
has been betrayed. Remember your responsibility is
to encourage and uplift them. You will do just the op-
posite if you betray their trust.

Be sincere. Be sincere. No one likes people who
are hypocrites and phony. People know whether you
are genuine or not. Do not pretend to be someone
you are not. Just offer to assist them as best you can

and stop there.

If you see they are drowning, get help for them.
Pay attention. It is normal for there to be mood, emotional and behavioral changes as people go through
the grieving process. For some, it is difficult to eat or
sleep and sometimes communicate. Although there is
no timetable for grief per se, this should only be tem-
porary. Eventually, you should see positive changes.
If not, and you see they are really struggling, encourage them to seek professional help.

Put yourself in their shoes. Make sure they are
treated with dignity and respect. Whether you have
personally faced a significant loss or not, chances are
you know how it feels to be mistreated. Don't do that
to someone else. Treat them in the same manner in
which you want to be treated.

Do not forget about them. Stay in touch. Oftentimes, when a death initially occurs, individuals are
flooded with family, friends, concerned neighbors
and co-workers. Generally, up to and including any
burial or memorial services, the survivors are sur-
rounded by people. However, after a few days or
weeks have passed, the phone and the doorbell stop
ringing; the condolences stop and the person is for all
practical purposes, left alone. In actuality, when you
are needed the most is often long after the services are
complete. Your assistance and encouragement will be

needed tomorrow, next week, next month, next year and for years to come.

The individual(s) you are assisting may choose to hold on to their grief and sorrow, but do not let that deter you from assisting them as best you can. Since different people often have different values, people will grieve differently. There is no cookie cutter grief pattern. As stated in a previous chapter, there are many factors that will determine the length of grieving as well as how successfully one moves through the grieving process. Do not become frustrated. Do your best to keep them focused and moving forward. Continue to work through the process with them. Utilize the practical applications, and you'll be surprised how you can and will make a difference.

For good order, let's review the practical ways you can help someone who is grieving:

- Remember the survivors
- Be a good listener
- Let them talk about their loved one
- Watch what you say
- Whatever you see that needs to be done, do it
- Visit them
- Call them
- Pray for them
- Send a card, personal letter or note
- Offer to take them somewhere
- Ask them how you can help
- Be a person they can trust
- Be sincere
- If you see they are drowning, get help for them
- Put yourself in their "shoes"
- Do not forget about them

Personal Notes

_____

_____

_____

_____

_____

_____

_____

_____

_____

_____

_____

Personal Notes

_____

_____

_____

_____

_____

_____

_____

_____

_____

_____

_____

Personal Notes

_____

_____

_____

_____

_____

_____

_____

_____

_____

_____

Part 4
Short-Term
Separation

Chapter 9

For The Believers

T he following chapter is devoted to those of Christian faith. If you prefer not to read the following information, please feel free to fast forward to the Epilogue. However, please keep in mind the insight, tools, and applications in this book can be used by everyone regardless of religious views or lack thereof.

For those who are Christians, there is great news: IT IS NOT THE END! Physical death is only a short-term separation. I Thessalonians 4:13-18 explains it beautifully.

"Now, concerning those who from time to time pass away, we would not have you to be ignorant, brethren, lest you should mourn as others do who have no hope. For if we believe that Jesus has died and risen again, we also believe that, through Jesus, God will bring with Him those who shall have

passed away. For this we declare to you on the Lord's own authority–that we who are alive and continue on earth until the Coming of the Lord, shall certainly not forestall those who shall have previously passed away. For the Lord Himself will come down from Heaven with a loud word of command, and with an archangel's voice and the trumpet of God, and the dead in Christ will rise first. Afterwards we who are alive and are still on earth will be caught up in their company amid clouds to meet the Lord in the air. And so we shall be with the Lord for ever. Therefore encourage one another with these words."
Weymouth's New Testament (WNT)

Look at verses 13, 14 and 16.

"Now, concerning those who from time to time pass away, we would not have you to be ignorant, brethren, lest you should mourn as others do who have no hope. For if we believe that Jesus has died and risen again, we also believe that, through Jesus, God will bring with Him those who shall have passed away. For the Lord Himself will come down from Heaven with a loud word of command, and with an archangel's voice and the trumpet of God, and the dead in Christ will rise first."

Let's read it again. This time, insert the name of your loved one:

Now, concerning **(insert your loved one's name)** who has passed away, I (Jesus) would not have you to be ignorant, lest you should mourn as others do who have no hope. For if you believe that I (Jesus) died and rose again, you should also believe that, through Me (Jesus), I will bring **(insert your loved one's name)** with me although he/she has passed away. For the Lord Himself will come down from Heaven with a loud word of command, and with an archangel's voice and the trumpet of God, and all those who have died, including **(insert your loved one's name)** will rise first.

Oh my; inserting their actual name gives brand new insight and illumination into this personal promise from our Father God to you, your loved one and all believers in Christ.

Let's keep reading; there is another jewel to point out; look at the second part of verse 18 again: *"...Therefore encourage one another with these words."* The King James Version says, *"...Therefore comfort one another with these words."*

Whether YOU believe these words are effective or not, the Word of God IS true.

"For the Word of God is quick and powerful and sharper than any two-edged sword, piercing even to the dividing asunder of soul and spirit, and of the joints and marrow, and is a discerner of the thoughts and intents of the heart." Hebrews 4:12

If God said these words will bring comfort and encouragement, then they will.

I have often heard people say, *"I just don't know what to say to someone,"* or *"It's so awkward."* Say what Jesus would say. Remind them they have hope and a promise from Almighty God, that physical death is not the end. The reason many people feel squeamish about saying this verse is because either they do not really believe it or they do not have a revelation of it. Your sympathy has limited power that is fleeting. However, the Word of God is filled with unlimited effectiveness.

Let's parallel being absent from home or a job with being absent from your body. Imagine you have a son or daughter that goes out of state to college and will not be home again until summer break. While you will miss your child, you are not devastated because you trust and believe that in a few months, you will see him or her again. Your child will be home for the summer. Maybe you have a son or daughter who goes to stay with Grandma for the summer. Even though you miss them terribly, you have hope that they will return in a few weeks.

What about those of you who either travel for your job or have a spouse who travels? Yes, they may be gone for a few days or weeks at a time, or you may be gone, still you have the expectation that you will see them again. You can still function and go on because you know it is not the end.

So it is when someone you love dies. IT IS NOT THE END. If someone you love dearly has passed from death to eternal life, whether they are deceased due to their body wearing out because of age, or they died some other way, you will see them again. When you know it is not the last time you will see someone, you are comforted. You realize it is just a matter of time before you see them again.

That is why this scripture gives comfort and encouragement. We do not sorrow as others who have no hope because we know, trust and believe WE WILL SEE THEM AGAIN. Let the church say, Amen!

ICING ON THE CAKE

If that scripture alone wasn't good enough, look at *John 11:25-26.*

"I am the Resurrection and the Life" said Jesus. "He who believes in me, even if he has died, he shall live; and every one who is living and is a believer in me shall never, never die. Do you believe this?" (WNT)

Wow, what a verse. After He made such a power-ful statement, He asked a simple question: *"Do you believe this?"* It is decision making time. You either believe that His Word is true or you do not. There is no middle ground. If you believe His Word, you will be able to comfort and encourage someone else, and you also will be comforted.

"I don't want to hear that."
Once at a funeral service I attended, one of the

family members was really sorrowing. She felt hope-less. She snapped and said to someone, "Don't tell me not to cry because I will see them again. I don't want to hear that." I thought to myself, that is exactly what you need to hear if you want to be comforted. She did not understand that the scripture indeed would bring her comfort. However in this instance, the deceased had accepted Christ, but the family member had not. As a result, she felt hopeless. She was not able to be comforted by this wonderful scripture because she had no reference point. In her case, all she could hold on to were her memories. But if you believe in Jesus Christ, you can hold on to the fact that you will be reunited in the not so distant future.

AN IMPORTANT NOTE

Stop trying to explain it.

Please stop trying to explain why a person died! We do not always know why things happen. We do not always understand why things happen. Even if God gave you a dissertation on why a loved one died, you would not be satisfied. You would ask more questions and want more answers. *"There remaineth there-fore a rest to the people of God." Hebrews 4:9.* Just rest in knowing, if you have received Jesus Christ as your personal Lord and Savior, and your loved one has as well, IT IS NOT THE END. You will see them again. "Do you believe this?"

"'I heard the voice from heaven saying, 'Write, Blessed are the dead who die in the Lord from now on.' 'Yes says the Spirit that they may rest from their labors; for their works follow with them.'" Rev. 14:13 (WEB)

The unborn child.

Many years ago, one of my husband's friends lost his sister and he was going to the memorial service. I thanked my husband for being such a supportive friend and he went his way. When my husband returned, I could tell he was a little disturbed. After inquiring what was wrong he explained. It turned out that the sister was pregnant. The baby who had been virtually carried to term had died also. As a result, there the mother lay in a casket, and the unborn, nine month old child in a tiny, beautiful, white coffin next to her. My husband had no idea he would see a beautiful little baby lying there so still as well.

You cannot explain why an innocent little baby died, so do not try to explain it. The parents, family and friends just have to support each other and do their best to keep their memory alive.

IN TIMES LIKE THESE

I am so excited to share *Psalm 46:1*. It is a wonderful scripture in times like these. *"God is our refuge and strength, a very present help in trouble."*

This scripture provides three perfect things:

1. God is our *refuge*; our shelter, our protection from danger or distress.

2. God is our *strength*; our support, our power, our firmness.

3. God is our *very present help in trouble*; ready at hand, quick in emergency, in view.

Another item for the Christians: HEAVEN

Revelation 21:10-27 describes the Holy City of Heaven. Heaven is enormous and beautiful. No words in any language could adequately describe its beauty. It is filled with the most precious and flawless stones known to mankind. The gold in Heaven is pure, without fillers or debris. The closest description of its appearance is like pure glass. There is no sickness, disease or death. Heaven only knows joy, peace, love and all good things. The mansions there would make the greatest architects and craftsmen we have ever known feel void of skills. It is filled with Praise and Worship to God Almighty and our blessed Lord and Savior; the precious Lamb of God-Jesus.

"Heaven Is Real."

Heaven is a REAL PLACE. It is not some figment of the imagination, or an obscure place that people talk about. Heaven is real. There are real people, unimaginable beauty and best of all, THE THRONE OF GOD. Do not feel sorry for someone who is in heaven.

They would NEVER want to stay here once they receive a glimpse of heaven. The peace and joy coupled with the continuous praise of the angels towards God are simply too much for our mortal minds to fathom. As Paul so eloquently stated: *"I do not count the sufferings of our present life worthy of mention when compared with the Glory that is to be revealed and bestowed upon us." Romans 8:18 (TCNT)*

"When they see the Light of Heaven."

I was recently visiting with one of my adopted daughters. We were discussing what happens when people get a glimpse of Heaven. As much as we would like to keep our loved ones with us, when they see the light of Heaven and hear angels singing, they almost always choose to leave earth, and join God in Heaven.

As we were talking, these words came out of my mouth: "Think of the most awesome spiritual experience you have ever had. Think of your most memorable time spent in the presence of the Lord. Think of how glorious it *felt*, and how you did not want that experience to end. Now, take that glorious experience and multiply it by a thousand. That's what happens when you get a glimpse of Heaven."

You are faced with the choice of staying here in your mortal body, or experiencing the non-stop presence and fullness of God. If you had that choice, which would you choose?

Many times when a loved one is making a decision to stay in the body or move to Heaven, we prolong their transition because of our personal needs and desires. We do not want them to leave us, so we hold onto them. Once we make a decision to let them go, they usually transition quickly. Remember, NOTHING compares to the Glory of God. The scripture is true, "...*to be absent from the body, is to be present with the Lord*" *(II Corinthians 5:8)*. Rest in knowing they are in a perfect place, fellowshipping with a perfect God. And, you will see them again.

"Behold, I shew you a mystery; We shall not all sleep, but we shall all be changed, In a moment, in the twinkling of an eye, at the last trump: for the trumpet shall sound, and the dead shall be raised incorruptible, and we shall be changed. For this corruptible must put on incorruption, and this mortal must put on immortality. So when this corruptible shall have put on immortality, then shall be brought to pass the saying that is written, Death is swallowed up in victory, O death, where is thy sting? O grave, where is thy victory?" I Corinthians 15:51-55

Praise God! The grave has no victory. Your loved one is in your FUTURE!

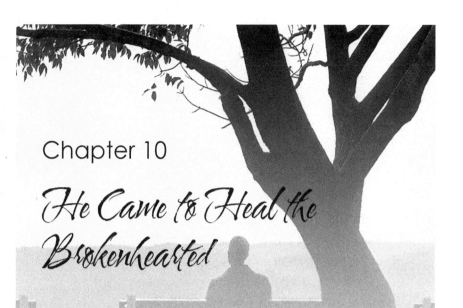

Chapter 10

He Came to Heal the Brokenhearted

Psalm 34:18
The Lord is nigh unto them that are of a broken heart; and saveth such as be of a contrite spirit.

Isaiah 61:1-3
The spirit of the Lord God is upon me; because the Lord hath anointed me to preach good tidings unto the meek; he hath sent me to bind up the brokenhearted, to proclaim liberty to the captives, and the opening of the prison to them that are bound; to proclaim the accept-able year of the Lord, and the day of vengeance of our God; to comfort all that mourn; to appoint unto them that mourn in Zion, to give unto them beauty for ashes, the oil of joy for

mourning, the garment of praise for the spirit of heaviness.

Luke 4:18-19
The Spirit of the Lord is upon me, because he hath anointed me to preach the gospel to the poor; he hath sent me to heal the broken-hearted, to preach deliverance to the captives, and recovering of sight to the blind, to set at liberty them that are bruised, to preach the acceptable year of the Lord.

Matthew 11:28
Come unto me, all ye that labour and are heavy laden, and I will give you rest.

Matthew 5:4
Blessed are they that mourn: for they shall be comforted.

Psalm 23:4
Yea, though I walk through the valley of the shadow of death, I will fear no evil: for thou art with me; thy rod and thy staff they comfort me.

Psalm 121:1-8

I WILL lift up mine eyes unto the hills, from whence cometh my help. My help cometh from the Lord, which made heaven and earth. He will not suffer thy foot to be moved: he that keepeth thee will not slumber. Behold, he that keepth Israel shall neither slumber nor sleep. The Lord is they keeper: the Lord is thy shade upon thy right hand.

The sun shall not smite thee by day, nor the moon by night. The Lord shall preserve thee from evil: he shall preserve thy soul. The Lord shall preserve thy going out and thy coming in from this time forth, and even for evermore.

Isaiah 41:10

Fear thou not; for I am with thee: be not dismayed; for I am thy God: I will strengthen thee; yea, I will help thee; yea, I will uphold thee with the right hand of my righteousness.

Many individuals have watched loved ones suffer the ravaging effects of cancer, the suddenness of a deadly heart attack; while others have seen aging parents suffer from dementia and not even recognize their own spouse or children. God will heal your broken heart if you allow Him to. Surrender your pain and heartache to Him.

Like a heavy weight fighter, life can deliver very severe blows. Those blows can leave you wounded, confused, disheartened and dismayed. If your heart is broken, bring all the pieces to Jesus. He came to heal the brokenhearted!

Frequently Asked Questions

Before we conclude this material, here are some frequently asked questions.

Q. "All I do is cry. Is that normal?"
A. It is normal, okay and even healthy to cry or weep. There is a time to weep. Crying brings a physical release of pressure. You will miss your loved one. It is okay to show human emotions. However, you cannot allow a spirit of grief to consume you. You must keep your emotions in balance. You may cry for a time, but the day and time should come when you cry less. Over time, you should begin to adjust to your altered life. Eventually you should move from *"All I do is cry"* to *"Some days I don't cry at all."*

Q. "I just can't seem to get over this loss, what should I do?"
A. Read and study this material over and over again; seek counseling, go to a support group, find some help.

Q. "Why am I so angry?"
A. There may be many reasons for your anger. Please see the Stages of Grief and the Obstacles to Grieving. You must work through your anger. Anger is a deadly emotion.

Q. "Is it okay to visit the gravesite?"
A. There is no right or wrong about visiting the gravesite of your loved one. The question you have to ask is, why are you visiting the gravesite? What is your purpose? You want to focus your time and attention on the good and positive memories of your loved one. The gravesite is a constant reminder of death. You are not dishonoring your loved one if you don't go to the grave and plant flowers or place wreaths or sit and visit. Honor was given when they were alive. If you focus on your loved one's death, it will be more difficult for you to move successfully through the grieving process.

On a personal note, I visit my mother's gravesite once or twice a year to ensure the lawn is manicured and that the grave is not disturbed because it is an old public cemetery with no maintenance personnel. I realize it is only her body in the grave. She is not there. I choose not to focus on her death, but on her life.

Q. "Why did this happen?"
A. There are many situations where the cause for death is known. However, there are many deaths that occur where you may never know the answer to that question. Even if you "know" why a person died, for example a car accident or cancer, there may still be questions of how the cancer was contracted or why the car veered off the road. Please see Stop Trying to explain it.

Q. "I have a shrine for my loved one in my home. Should I remove it?"
A. You may choose to have comforting reminders of your loved one. Notice the word *comforting*. If the items on display keep you depressed and in a state of grief, pack them up and put them away for safe-keeping. If the items are so numerous you can barely move around the house, please remove them. Also, consider others

who will see your "shrine." Other family members or loved ones may not be strong enough to handle the constant visible reminders.

Final Thoughts: Epilogue

A fter reading through this material, it is our hope that something you have read has helped you, or will help you in the future, to get through the pain and sorrow associated with a significant loss. Unlike cars, jobs, houses, money and other material possessions, people cannot be replaced.

Whether you are going through the stages of grief or helping someone who is, please know you will have brighter days ahead. "The sun will come out tomorrow." It has been said, "Time heals all wounds." That is not necessarily true. There are multitudes of individuals still carrying hurts, wounds and offenses from their past. Many go months, years, decades and some even die, never recovering from the pain and sorrow brought about as a result of a significant loss, hurt or offense. Time does help heal wounds if you create an environment or atmosphere for the wound to heal. Physical wounds and scars can certainly heal themselves. The human body was designed by God to heal itself. On the other hand, emotional wounds and scars do not just disappear. They must be driven away. You may ask, "How do I drive my hurt away? What do I need to do?" I believe the following steps will help you:

Create an environment or atmosphere for healing to take place. For example, make a list of daily actions or activities you will do. Maybe your plan of action will be to daily begin speaking positive words over the situation. Start by saying, *"I forgive my uncle for molesting me as a child"* (or name whoever/whatever has caused the hurt). ***Please don't say it out loud if there are others around you or scream it to the person.** If they are alive, confrontation may come later after you have reached a certain level of personal healing. You may also want to say, *"I release the hurt and pain that (**insert the name**) caused me"* or *"I am angry because (**insert the name**) died, but I am determined not to wallow in my anger."* Notice, you have to say something to get the ball rolling. Once you speak it, eventually you will be motivated to put action behind the words you are speaking. Keep in mind the focus is on YOU, not them.

Good information. Research as much information as you can on releasing hurt, grief, forgiveness and any other areas of struggle. If that task seems too difficult a challenge for you, ask your personal support system to get the information for you. If you or they have internet access, the information is virtually endless on any subject and right at your fingertips. If you do not have access, the library is a great resource for information as well.

Self determination. While others can do the best they can to motivate you and cheer you onward, success ultimately rests with only one person-YOU. You must do all you can to stay focused on the goal of releasing the sorrow of grief. No one can do it for you.

Proper support. As mentioned previously, allow others to help you if available. There may be days you may feel as if this whole process is too difficult for you. You may feel you are not strong enough or ready to confront the source of your pain and sorrow, but you must confront it. Ask for help.

Make a quality decision to release the hurt TODAY. You cannot allow the sorrow of grief to fester. You must desire and strive to be free from the hurt and pain associated with a significant loss. That does not mean all your feelings will cease and vanish away. They will not. It simply means that the pain, sorrow and sting of the loss are significantly reduced as you go through life.

The materials covered in this resource will certainly help you successfully navigate your sunless skies if you apply them. No one will ever be able to take the place of your loved one. However, you can and should continue to lead a productive, positive life as you remember the life of your loved one. Once you have reached a level of healing in this area, it is our prayer that you will reach out and help someone else. Decide today to live again.

Personal Notes

_____

_____

_____

_____

_____

_____

_____

_____

_____

_____

_____

_____

Personal Notes

Personal Notes

_____

_____

_____

_____

_____

_____

_____

_____

_____

_____

_____

Appendices, References, & Resources

APPENDIX A
The Prayer to Receive Jesus Christ Into Your Heart

"But what saith it? The word is nigh thee, even in thy mouth, and in thy heart: that is, the word of faith, which we preach; That if thou shalt confess with thy mouth the Lord Jesus, and shalt believe in thine heart that God hath raised Him from the dead, thou shalt be saved. For with the heart man believeth unto righteousness; and with the mouth confession is made unto salvation. For the scripture saith, Whosoever believeth on Him shall not be ashamed. For there is no difference between the Jew and the Greek: for the same Lord over all is rich unto all that call upon Him. For whosoever shall call upon the name of the Lord shall be saved" (Romans 10:8-13).

Pray this Prayer:
"Dear Lord Jesus, please come into my heart and save me. Please forgive me of my sins. With Your

help, I turn away from sin. I believe You died for me and I believe You rose again. You said if I believed in my heart, and confessed with my mouth, I would be saved. I believe in my heart, and I confess with my mouth that You are Lord. Help me to learn more about You and Your plan for my life. In Jesus' Name, Amen."

It is that simple. People make it complicated, God makes it simple. Now that you have made the most important decision of your life, make sure you find a good Bible-believing, Bible-teaching church. A good church will help you develop and grow into the amazing person God created you to be.

What is a good "Bible-believing, Bible-teaching church?" I'm glad you asked. A Bible-believing, Bible-teaching church is one where the Bible is taught as the infallible Word of God. The messages should be clear, easy to understand, and based on the Scriptures, not someone's personal opinion.

You should be taught the Word of God (the Bible), and encouraged to read it for yourself. Although the pastor should be teaching you godly principles at church, you have a responsibility to read and study the Bible for yourself. When you have questions, you should be able to ask the pastor or a designated minister or a designated parishioner for assistance. Do not ask your neighbor. Ask someone from the church staff. If the messages you hear are not helping you be a better person, as well as help you turn away from an ungodly lifestyle, or if only your emotions are stirred up, you need to keep looking. There are wonderful Bible-believing, Bible-teaching churches around. You will find one you enjoy!

One note on finding a good church: NO CHURCH IS PERFECT! Why is that? Because a church is filled with people, and people have issues; some more than others, and some more dramatic than others; besides that, you are there. You are not perfect, and neither is the pastor or the other members who attend. Be patient and make a decision that any church you join, you will be an asset, not a liability.

APPENDIX B
Self-Help Worksheet

1. Identify the stage(s) of grief that best describe you today (select all that apply).

○ Shock
○ Emotional "dysfunction"
○ Depression, loneliness
○ Physical symptoms
○ A sense of guilt
○ Anger or rage
○ Difficulty or inability to return to usual activities
○ Gradual adjustment to your "altered" life
○ Acceptance of your "altered" life

2. From the list below, select those helps that you currently utilize (select all that apply).

○ Acknowledgement
○ Talk it out
○ Do not try to go it alone
○ Listen
○ Do not be in denial
○ Take care of your body
○ Surround yourself with positive people
○ Use a journal
○ Set up a support system
○ Get out of the house

○ Read your condolences
○ Do not isolate yourself
○ Help and encourage someone else
○ Join a support group
○ Talk to your Priest, Pastor or Professional
   Counselor
○ Forgive yourself
○ Forgive others
○ Give yourself time to heal

3. From the list below, select those helps you are not currently using that you believe will help you (select all that apply).

○ Acknowledgement
○ Talk it out
○ Do not try to go it alone
○ Listen
○ Do not be in denial
○ Take care of your body
○ Surround yourself with positive people
○ Use a journal
○ Set up a support system
○ Get out of the house
○ Read your condolences
○ Do not isolate yourself
○ Help and encourage someone else
○ Join a support group
○ Talk to your Priest, Pastor or Professional
   Counselor

○ Forgive yourself
○ Forgive others
○ Give yourself time to heal

4. How can you implement the above helps into your healing process?

5. Additional ways you can help yourself:

6. Will you make a decision and commit to start today? ○ YES   ○ NO

Quotes of Interest

"Some people grieve because they have lost a pet, a job, a dream or a relationship." (Page 15)

"You can work through your feelings of loss." (Page 16)

"Do not allow guilt to consume you." (Page 29)

"Fear will keep you from moving forward." (Page 31)

"There is no timetable for grief." (Page 37)

"Recognize when grief hits you." (Page 41)

"People who are grieving need encouragement, support and reassurance." (Page 74)

"There is no cookie cutter grief pattern." (Page 81)

ENDNOTES

Colbert, Don MD. *Stress Less.* (2008) Siloam Publishing. Lake Mary, FL.

Cooke, Tony, *Life after Death*, (2003) Faith Library Publications, Tulsa, OK.

CNN, *29 Killed in plane crash near Detroit,* January 9, 1997.

Family Caregiver Alliance. *Supporting Someone Who is Grieving,* Retrieval date: February 10, 2011.

Forgive to Live, PsychologyToday.com, (University of Tennessee Study, July 1, 2000) Retrieval date: April 5, 2011.

Health Benefits of Sleep, longevity.about.com, Mark Stibich, Ph.D., (2008) Retrieval date: August 30, 2011.

Kubler-Ross, Elizabeth, M.D. *On Death and Dying The Five Stages of Grief* (1997) Scribner Classics, New York, NY.

Merton, Robert K., *Social Theory and Social Structure, Self-fulfilling Prophecy,* (1968), The Free Press, Division of Simon and Schuster, Inc.

Noah Webster's *1828 American Dictionary of the English Language*.

Obstacles to Grieving, everydayhealth.com, Retrieval date: July 26, 2011.

The 7 Healthy Wonders of Water. WebMD© Retrieval date: March 1, 2010.

Death Statistics, Griefspeaks.com, Retrieval date: August 3, 2012.

John Donne, *No Man is an Island*, Poemhunter.com, Retrieval date: April 12, 2013.

Erich Fromm quotes, Goodreads.com. Retrieval date: July 30, 2011.

All Scripture quotations in this book are taken from the *King James Version (KJV)* of the Holy Bible.

Scripture quotations marked TCNT, WEB and WNT are taken from the Power BibleCD©.

Scripture Key (abbreviations)
KJV-King James Version
TCNT-Twentieth Century New Testament
WNT-Weymouth's New Testament
WEB-World English Bible

HELPFUL RESOURCES

Caring Connections
www.caringinfo.org
800-658-8898

Family Caregiver Alliance
www.caregiver.org
800-445-8106

New Life Ministries
www.newlife.com
800-NEW-LIFE

Everyday Health
www.everydayhealth.com

Grief Speaks
www.griefspeaks.com
973-912-0177

AARP
www.aarp.com
888.687.2277

Recommended Reading

Glimpses of Heaven: True Stories of Hope and Peace at the End of Life's Journey, Trudy Harris

Sorrow Not, Kenneth Copeland

Overcoming the Spirit of Grief, Keith A. Butler

Heaven: Close Encounters of the God Kind, Jesse Duplantis

My Glimpse of Eternity, Betty Multz

I Went to Hell, Kenneth E. Hagin

Life After Death: Rediscovering Life After the Loss of a Loved One, Tony Cooke

Redeemed from Shame, Denise Renner

Within Heavens Gates, Rebecca Springer

23 Minutes in Hell, Bill Wiese

Healing is a Choice, Stephen Arterburn

Live Again, Tracy Boyd

On Death and Dying:The Five Stages of Grief, Elizabeth Kubler-Ross

About the Author

Rosetta Archer is uniquely qualified for writing this critical resource. She has studied the *psyche*, the "breath, spirit, and soul" of mankind. Armed with a Social Science degree, with a concentration in Psychology, she is a Michigan State University graduate equipped to tackle the very personal and sensitive issues of human behavior during times of grief. Drawing from her years of experience and through the use of knowledge of the principles contained in this book, she has ministered to hundreds of grieving individuals, and those who desire to assist them.

Rosetta is a gifted psalmist, dynamic minister, and anointed author with a unique ability for addressing the challenges of life in a way that is easy to understand and apply to everyday life. An honor's graduate of the Word of Faith International Christian Center's Ministers Training Program, she brings the compassion in her heart for others to all the works that she embraces. Having traveled throughout the continental U.S. and abroad, she is also known internationally as a worship leader and singer. One of her fondest memories is traveling to Israel and leading several hundred ministers, leaders and laity in praise and worship on beautiful Mount Zion.

Rosetta and her husband of 29 years currently reside in the state of Michigan.

FOR MORE INFORMATION

If you would like to contact the author,
you may do so at:

Rosetta Archer
P.O. Box 7794
Bloomfield Hills, MI 48302
Sunless.skies@gmail.com

You may also contact Rosetta on the web:
www.SunlessSkies.com

Follow her on Facebook and Twitter
Facebook.com/SunlessSkies
Twitter.com/SunlessSK

SPREAD THE WORD

If this information has been helpful and beneficial to
you, spread the word.

Purchase additional copies and give them away to
family and friends. A gift of help and hope will last a
lifetime.

Additional copies may be purchased at:
www.SunlessSkies.com & www.amazon.com
Available on eBook, too
*For bulk purchases, please go to www.SunlessSkies.com or
call 248.346.3605*